The Gaze of Indifference

초판 1쇄 발행 2023년 05월 11일

지은이 Jayun Choi

펴낸이 김동명 **펴낸곳** 도서출판 창조와 지식 **인쇄처** (주)북모아

출판등록번호 제2018-000027호

주소 서울특별시 강북구 덕릉로 144

전화 1644-1814 **팩스** 02-2275-8577

ISBN 979-11-6003-556-8

정가 8,500원

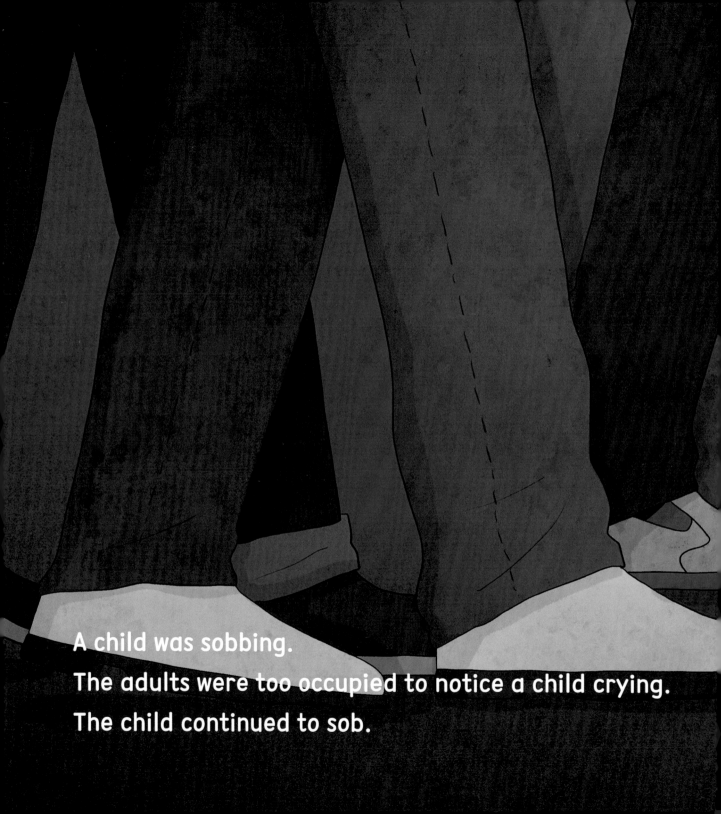

A child was sobbing.

The adults were too occupied to notice a child crying.

The child continued to sob.

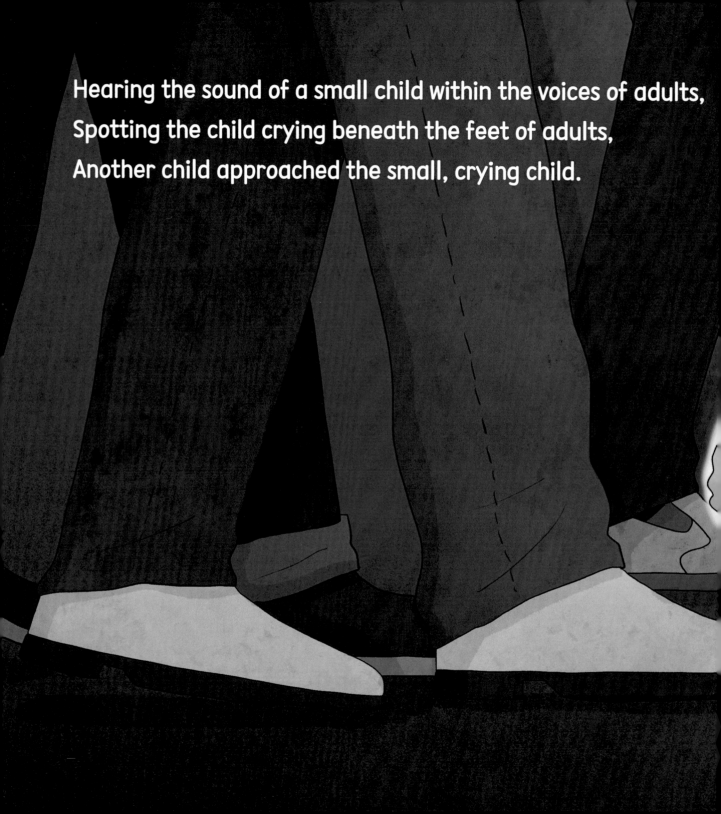

Hearing the sound of a small child within the voices of adults,
Spotting the child crying beneath the feet of adults,
Another child approached the small, crying child.

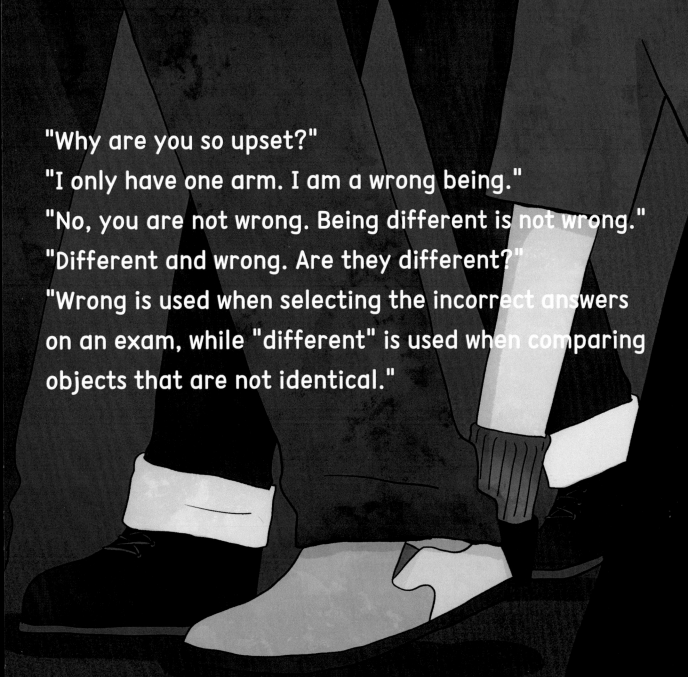

"Why are you so upset?"

"I only have one arm. I am a wrong being."

"No, you are not wrong. Being different is not wrong."

"Different and wrong. Are they different?"

"Wrong is used when selecting the incorrect answers on an exam, while "different" is used when comparing objects that are not identical."

"My teacher told me that being different makes all of us precious beings."

"So you are not wrong. You are just different."

"Then I am not socially erroneous. I'm distinct."

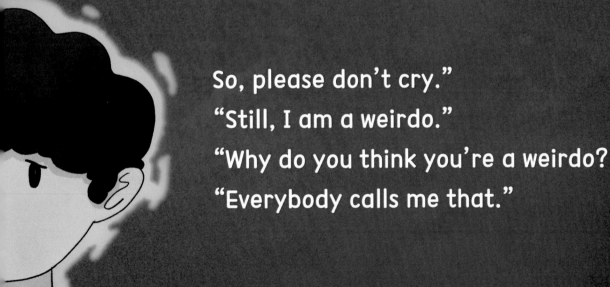

So, please don't cry."

"Still, I am a weirdo."

"Why do you think you're a weirdo?

"Everybody calls me that."

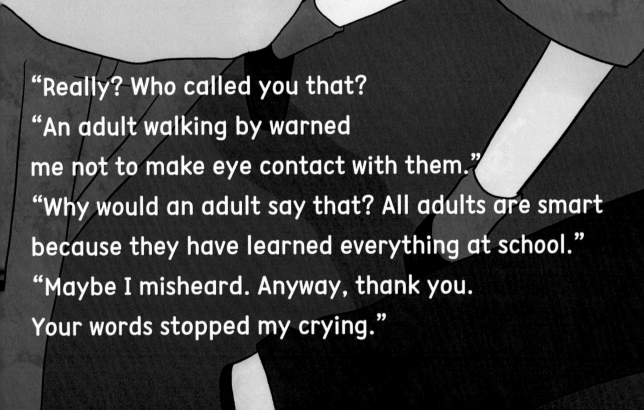

"Really? Who called you that?
"An adult walking by warned
me not to make eye contact with them."
"Why would an adult say that? All adults are smart
because they have learned everything at school."
"Maybe I misheard. Anyway, thank you.
Your words stopped my crying."

For a brief moment, a child's sobbing stopped.
The child who assisted a child smiled and
walked away.
However, the crying ceased for a moment.
Again, a child began to cry.

A child's cries were unheard and never reached the child.
The child forgot the memories of him and a crying child.
The child ignored and compromised with society,
just like other adults.

Like other adults, the child had a loving kid.
The kid resembled the child very much.
The kid was also interested in helping crying children.

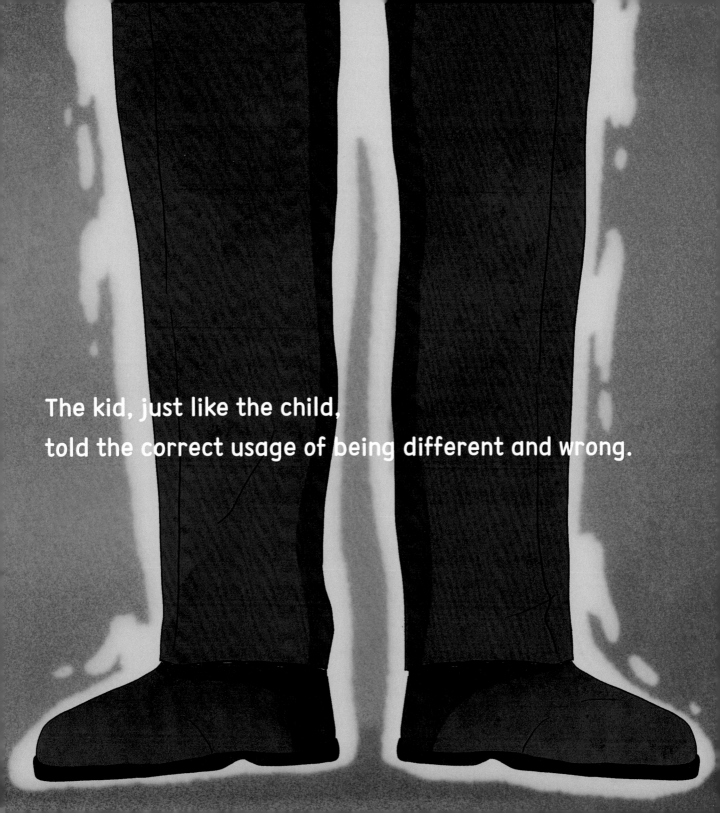

The kid, just like the child,
told the correct usage of being different and wrong.

Too occupied with success,
the child forgot to look back or down.

One day, the child and the kid went for a walk.
The kid heard the cries.
But the child could not.